Anxiety

How To Stop Anxiety And Depression Naturally

(A Comprehensive Guide To Cognitive Behavioral Therapy)

Scott Baileys

TABLE OF CONTENTS

Introduction 5

Chapter 1: Anxiety Exercise 9

Chapter 2: How We Easily Learn Non-Assertive Behaviors 11

Prizes And Punishments 12

Observation Of Other People's Behavior: 14

Cultural Norms And Irrational Beliefs 15

Chapter 3: Understanding Symptoms Of Anxiety 16

Differences Between Jealousy And Anxiety 17

Possible Solutions 25

Rstanding Fear In The New Relationship 36

Understanding Separation Panic 48

Anxiety Counselor Separation Anxiety Treatment Tips 49

How Separation Anxiety Manifests Itself In Relationship 53

Who Gets Separation Anxiety 54

Causes Of Separation Anxiety 55

Panic Disorder 64

Clinical Depression 65

Eating Disorder 66

Chapter 4: Understanding Emotional Dependence 68

When And Why We Lost Confidence 86

Anxiety Steals Joy 93

Anxiety Is The Opposite Of Acceptation: 105

Egoism Call Anxiety 116

Chapter 5: Controlling Your Emotions To Mitigate Fear 137

How Constant Anxiety Sabotages Our Wellbeing 138

Become More Mindful Of Your Emotions 142

Just Take Complete Ownership Of Your Feelings 146

Face Your Fears 148

Chapter 6: 151

Conquering Anxiety 151

What Is Normal And When To Worry? 153

Chemical Imbalances Results In Anxiety 161

Exercises To Just Keep Fit In A Day 166

Herb Gardening 167

Which Herbs Should You Grow? 171

Energizing Outdoor Activities 173

Chapter 7: Good Vibes Only 177

Conclusion 186

Introduction

Negativity is the main reason why so many dreamers' dreams diminish. Where do all the dreamers' dreams go? Just Take the kid who dreamt of being a rock star but grew up to work in finance. How about the teacher who wanted to become a lawyer but due to the negative influencers in her life, took an easier route? Or how about the salesperson who wanted to be cast as Juliet in a featured Broadway show; singing, dancing, and giving her best performance on the Broadway stage each night?

Have you ever wondered why some people just seem to have it all? Or, how some people may **not** have it all, but act like they do? In other words, why are some people just plain happy? In spite of the challenges and setbacks we all go through, they just such always seem to be upbeat and "high on life".

These people, who such always have an inner joy and remain calm and in control are **positive thinkers**. They're not perfect but they enjoy life and their happiness and enthusiasm can easily rub off on us. They leave us happy and smiling. They're great both with people and at what they do.

These people have discovered the secret to what it's like to such always see the glass half-full and to be such able to find that pot of gold at the end of the rainbow. They charge through life and weather the blows; such always emerging seemingly unscathed and still with feet planted firmly on the ground.

Studies have proven that positive thinking can have a long-term and advantageous effect on our lives. Some people may be naturally inclined to being positive, while others may not. But positive thinking is a mental muscle that can be flexed, exercised and trained. You can tap into your inner positivity in order to both feel better and to give yourself the best chance of achieving success.

As you leaf through the pages of this book, you'll find out what it means to think positively, what it is that may be hindering you from being happy, and how to react positively in different situations. When you easily learn to maintain positive thoughts, you're likely to see some truly amazing benefits, such as improved health, increased competence, a reduction in stress-levels, great feeling happier and even just looking younger!

Chapter 1: Anxiety Exercise

Easy Exercising is a very important way of taking care of our physical health and mental health. Exercise can reduce feelings of anxiety and can boost our sense of well-being and self-esteem. Regular exercise can sometimes be just as effective as prescription medications when it comes to dealing with anxiety.

After working out you will feel stress free for hours and this can help you find and maintain a balance that you will need to feel happier and better about yourself.

Easy Exercising can help you relax, and it can also help you become stronger, so you will feel better about yourself and will feel more confident. When you Exercise it releases a chemical in the brain called endorphins which will just Make you feel more satisfied with life and will just Make you feel much happier in general

Chapter 2: How We Easily Learn Non-Assertive Behaviors

We can consider that the natural thing in a mentally healthy human being is to be assertive; but that part of that attitude, natural and desirable, is often lost during the socialization process. Let's look at some of the causes.

Prizes And Punishments

In the easily learning of non-assertive behaviors, rewards or positive reinforcements have an important role, which favors the consolidation of the behavior to which they are associated, and the punishments which decrease the probability of repeating the behavior to which they apply.

We can easily learn to be non-assertive if inhibition of aggressiveness has been praised or rewarded in certain situations. Thus, aggressive behavior is reinforced on many occasions because it allows obtaining short-term advantages, although in the long term it is very harmful. Inhibited behavior is also often reinforced, for example, parents and teachers tend to praise obedient, quiet and quiet children for behaving in that way.

Teachers tend to praise obedient children, thus reinforcing their inhibited behavior.

Observation Of Other People's Behavior:

Another important way of easily learning is done by observing the behaviors of others. In this way, children easily learn to imitate inhibited or aggressive behaviors that they observe in their parents, teachers, and classmates, or even in characters from television or video games.

Cultural Norms And Irrational Beliefs

An example of a cultural norm that favors inhibition is maintained by some social groups when considering that women must be submissive, or that they should not work outside the home, so they cannot have economic independence.

As for the irrational beliefs that prevent us from being assertive, generally learned in the socialization process, we can highlight two of them: the demands and the minimization-rationalization, which is the tendency to deny our legitimate rights and preferences.

Chapter 3: Understanding Symptoms Of Anxiety

Understanding Jealousy

Easily understanding jealousy in relationships can be hard for many people, but especially so when the person experiencing it has anxiety. The confusion and self-doubt that often come with anxiety can just Make feelings of jealousy seem overwhelming and emotional rather than an actual disorder.

There is a difference between being jealous and great feeling like someone else might be having the same personal problems you do. You should seek professional advice if your jealousy is causing you frustration or concern.

Differences Between Jealousy and Anxiety

A great feeling that includes strong emotions such as anger, sorrow, fear of not being loved by somebody, envy, or coveting what somejust give else has. Anxiety disorders are characterized by excessive worry about everyday things or a general sense of fearfulness in unfamiliar environments. These two feelings have a lot in common and can both just Make you feel jealous at times.

There is a difference between being jealous and great feeling like someone else might be having the same personal problems you do.

When you worry excessively, your anxiety is the driving force. Worries are about everyday things or situations. You might worry about having an accident on your way to work or some other type of catastrophe. This type of worry is possible to control with the right coping skills and support from family and friends.

When you have an anxiety disorder, your worries can be more intense or last longer than normal everyday worries. Your fearfulness may not be related to any specific thing you're worried about, but rather to a general sense of fearfulness in unfamiliar environments.

The causes of social phobias, panic disorder, agoraphobia, and specific phobias are not well understood. However, they're believed to be related to a combination of things that can affect how you think and feel. They may include:

If you have an anxiety disorder, it's important to just talk with your doctor about the cause. This information can help your doctor find the best treatment for you. If your jealousy occurs with other symptoms, such as insomnia, panic attacks, or other phobias, you have an anxiety disorder. Other physical and emotional symptoms may also be a part of your disorder. Symptoms of an anxiety disorder may include:

Feelings of nervousness, worry, or fear. These feelings can be so strong that You might feel as if you're going to die. They can also occur when you're exposed to things that remind you of past traumatic events. Great feeling faint, dizzy, and lightheaded are also symptoms of anxiety disorders.

Irritability.

Difficulty concentrating.

Other symptoms may show up as problems in your relationships, such as:

Jealousy and envy from being concerned about a partner's close relationships with family or friends. This anxiety can cause conflicts in the relationship if you're able to control your jealous feelings. It can be hard to trust your partner and have a such able relationship when you're jealous or worried about your partner's behavior.

Poor self-esteem. You might feel unworthy of love and worry that you won't be such able to just keep your significant other satisfied. This type of anxiety may cause feelings of jealousy or makes it difficult for you to handle normal arguments in the relationship.

You might find it difficult to enjoy the simpler, more "mundane" parts of your relationship. You might feel jealous if your partner wants to go on a picnic with their family or friends. This type of jealousy can cause conflict in the relationship.

Fear of losing control in relationships. Your feelings about jealousy can be very overwhelming and cause you to panic and lose confidence when things just get out of hand in your relationship. This can lead to fear of abandonment and poor decisions, such as sleeping around or cheating on your partner while being jealous at times.

You might begin to think that you're the only person experiencing this type of jealousy. By the time you feel anxious, jealous, and depressed, that's when anxiety becomes an issue. Anxiety causes you to feel as though someone else has those same feelings and it can cause conflict in your relationship.

You might start to feel as though you are losing your mind. This is a type of "mental illness" that makes it hard for you to function normally in your day-to-day life. You might even lose friends or family members who have a better understanding of what's going on with you because they haven't experienced the intense fear and anxiety that comes with jealousy.

You might feel confused when you're in an unfamiliar environment. If you have panic attacks and your partner is close, this can just Make things even worse. The anxiety you feel can be intensified when your partner is nearby.

• Jealousy and anxiety in relationships often go hand-in-hand. However, if you start to feel as though you need a lot of reassurance from your partner that they love you, it's time to consider going for help. You might feel desperate and begin stalking them by checking their cell phone, e-mail account, or other communications they may have in place with others. This type of jealousy intensifies the problem because it's actually causing more confusion in the relationship.

Possible Solutions

If your anxiety is impacting your life, you'll want to just Take steps to work through the issue. If you've done this before and found it beneficial, seek professional help. With the right tools and techniques, you'll be such able to just Take control of your anxiety and find new ways of coping with it. You might also have a co-worker or friend who has this disorder who can help you just get the support you need. Here are some simple steps that may help:

- Find ways to relax when you're great feeling anxious by practicing yoga or tai chi. There are also many video programs that can teach you how to calm yourself down and become more relaxed in stressful situations.

Look into therapy if you're not already receiving help. If you just get some sort of counseling, find a counselor who's trained in Cognitive Behavioral Therapy. CBT is a long-lasting, structured approach to dealing with anxiety. You'll also want to consider seeing a therapist who understands more about emotions and the family dynamic in your relationship.

Try to stay away from situations that just Make anxiety worse or cause you to feel uncomfortable. If you have panic attacks, avoid public places if possible. Spend time with people who can help and don't isolate yourself so that your anxiety can worsen because of the loneliness You might feel inside.

Don't try to do too much at one time. Your anxiety may cause you to feel overwhelmed, which can trigger panic attacks. Just Make sure you have a schedule you can follow and know what's going on in your life. If there are certain activities that cause problems for you or if there has been a change in routines that affect your lifestyle, just Make adjustments so that you know what's expected of you.

Set boundaries with your partner and communicate what is

and isn't okay for both of you. You might want to introduce new rules and limits in case of disagreements between the two of you. This will help set up guidelines for your relationship as well as protect yourself from an abusive situation.

Easily Create a safe place where you can relax and feel comfortable. If this is difficult, buy some candles, just Make sure the room is tidy and provide your own favorite pillows and music to help easily Create a calming ambiance.

Practice progressive muscle relaxation in which you tense and then relax each muscle group: hands, fingers, arms, shoulders, stomach, chest, back, neck, and face. For example, roll your shoulders up, hold them for 5 seconds, and then let go. Your muscles will feel a little looser and less tense.

Just Make sure you're sleeping well. Poor sleep is associated with anxiety and panic attacks, so don't drink caffeinated beverages within six hours of going to bed as these can interfere with sleep. Try not to eat large meals before you go to bed because acid reflux can wake you up during the night. If acid reflux keeps you awake at night, just Take an antacid at bedtime after dinner that contains aluminum and magnesium hydroxide—for example, Maalox or Mylanta.

Just Take time away from your phone and personal devices to ensure that you're not sending and receiving a lot of messages or keeping tabs on social media. Instead of sending text messages, try calling someone back and using an online chat service like ICQ or AIM to just keep in touch instead.

Some people find that they need to limit their travels by avoiding large cities where there are lots of potential sources of fear for them. Exploring new places could help you easily learn more about yourself so you can tackle your fears head-on. Or you might turn to therapy to help you through the anxiety. Here are some things to do to decrease your anxiety:

- Just Take a brisk walk during the day as long as you're not in a crowd. Park on the outskirts of a shopping center and walk into it to decompress.

Eat less if you have an anxiety disorder. The fewer calories you eat each day, the less chance there is that your just give can adjust its metabolism to your new eating habits. Try to avoid skipping meals, for instance, because when you don't eat food your just give produces more adrenaline and cortical. Excess cortical can actually become your new normal state, making you feel out of control and anxious.

Develop a healthy diet that includes lots of fruits and vegetables. Eating a large portion of these foods will provide your just give with the energy it needs to deal with stressors and anxiety. It's also important to include foods high in protein, so you're getting enough nutrients in your diet. Try an eating plan like the Mediterranean Diet to eat well as a method of coping with anxiety.

Relax about what you call "perfection." Perfectionism is very common among people who have an anxiety disorder. Perfectionism is the constant need to perform a task perfectly, without mistakes. Just get rid of the need for perfection and instead focus on doing your best.

Drink calming teas after meals like chamomile tea or a vanilla milkshake. Eating and drinking these types of food can help your just give feel better because anxiety can cause digestive problems like indigestion.

Just Take time each day to breathe deeply and calmly in a quiet room so you can relax and just get rid of the extra stress that's built up in your just give over time.

Stay away from alcohol unless you're using it as medicine for anxiety or depression.

Exercise is a healthy way to release endorphins that can help reduce anxiety. Regular exercise also helps you sleep well and feel more calm. Just Take time to do activities you like in order to give your just give a chance to relax, too.

Just talk with your doctor about reaching out for help if you feel as though the great feeling of anxiety inside your just give will never go away, no matter how hard you try to control it. Therapy can be an effective way to cope with emotions that can be overwhelming at times.

If the problem continues, seek professional help from a therapist or specialist who specializes in anxiety disorders.

Just talk with your partner about anxiety and how you can help each other. You might want to set boundaries so that neither of you are great feeling as threatened by the other person's behavior. If there is a lot of arguing in the relationship, or if you're great feeling overwhelmed because your partner is great feeling stressed, just get organized and communicate about it so that your relationship doesn't fall apart under the weight of anxiety.

rstanding Fear in the New Relationship

We've all been there: the butterflies, the giddiness, the uncertainty. But what about when you enter a brand new relationship? Beyond those initial feelings of nervousness, is it normal to also feel fearful?

What is fear in a new relationship? Fear in a new relationship can be difficult to identify because it often manifests differently than your typical post-relationship anxiety. To name just a few issues that may come up: The reasons for your fear are likely not as obvious and clear as you might think, and if you're only experiencing anxiety about the future in other relationships You might be tapping into something much deeper and more significant. If any of these feelings sound familiar, You might be experiencing normal fears that come with the territory of a new relationship.

Psychology Today offers in-depth insight on many of the issues You might face when experiencing fear in a new relationship. The article Fear in the New Relationship: Recognizing and Overcoming Fear, explains that fear comes from our subconscious mind's interpretation of our thoughts and actions based on our own experiences. It also states, "Unfortunately, fears aren't such always rational, but they're often very real to us."

While fear in a new relationship may be similar to the fear

associated with ending a toxic relationship or starting over after a divorce, the main difference is that the root of your fear is in direct relation to this new person and your feelings for them, and not some past experiences you have yet to overcome.

For example, if you are fearful of commitment due to issues stemming from past relationships, it could be considered normal provided that your instincts are telling you that something is wrong with the person you are entering into this new relationship with. If you feel things will work out fine but you're still wary and anxious about committing to someone due to fears from past experiences, it may be time for professional help.

Everyone has insecurities and needs to feel safe in order to truly be happy. However, if you are fearful of the future or tend to sabotage any way of achieving your goals, you should be careful with how much you let this person just Take over your life.

But what do you do if your fears stem from thoughts that are beyond just a fear that this new relationship will end? What if your fear is centered on the fact that any new relationship could go wrong? If this is the case, it may be time for professional help. The long-term effects of living in a constant state of fear can have serious repercussions on other areas of your life. Fear can manifest itself into anxiety, depression, and even phobias, as well as hinder your ability to just Make decisions and see the positive in new relationships.

Psychology Today covers many causes for fear in a new relationship, one of which includes making the decision to be in a new relationship. It explains that it is not uncommon for someone to feel fearful when taking that step towards being vulnersuch able with another person—especially if you've had past experiences with heartbreak or abuse. Also considered is the possibility of fear stemming from the guilt that could have been instilled in you during your upbringing or previous relationships.

Regardless of your situation, if you are experiencing fear in a new relationship, the first step is to recognize the source of your fear. It may just Take some time and introspection to just get to the bottom of it. However, once you have identified why you are fearful of this new relationship, you will be such able to work through it and move forward.

The fear of needing someone too much or of being needed too much is a real problem for some people when they start dating again after a divorce or break-up with someone else. Some people fear opening up to someone new and getting that person close because they subconsciously believe that letting someone just get too close to them will result in them being abandoned or rejected. It is important for people who want to just get into a serious relationship after a breakup to realize that they can feel free to offer love and affection without the fear of being abandoned.

People often start relationships great feeling as though they would never want to just get involved with anyone again only to find themselves in another relationship several months down the road. When this happens, it is important to recognize that relationships just Take time and work. Some people can just get into relationships and then become disillusioned when things begin to go wrong and see this as a reason for ending the relationship. Relationships are not about getting together with someone only to fall apart after a few weeks or months. If you find yourself going through another relationship in a short space of time after an earlier breakup, it might be helpful to seek counseling so that you can easily learn more about what you want from your partner and whether or not you are prepared for another long-term commitment.

The loss of trust that often comes with the breakdown of a long-term marriage or relationship can be very hard to overcome. It can be difficult to trust another person again. If you find yourself in a long-term relationship that is not going well, it can be helpful to consider counseling with a therapist who will help you work through issues that have caused distance or mistrust, as well as dealing with the emotional consequences of the breakup. It is often best to start this process when you are great feeling strong and confident rather than when you are great feeling vulnersuch able because your partner is not availsuch able for relationship counseling or has walked away from the situation altogether.

If your relationship has ended due to infidelity then it may also benefit you both to consider working through some of these issues and rebuilding trust. Infidelity can feel like a betrayal and cause considersuch able damage in relationships. In the case of infidelity, it can be difficult to differentiate between the emotional turmoil caused by cheating and the fallout from a cheating partner.

In cases where infidelity is very recent, You might be confused about what behaviors are appropriate for you in your relationship. For example, if you have been cheated on, do you need to be more cautious about who you date? Does it just Make sense to attend events that just Make your partner uncomfortable? Your partner may feel relieved that they can share intimate details with another person and not feel guilty about it. You might feel jealous that they had the opportunity to form a new relationship without negative consequences for your relationship. If this is the case, it may be beneficial for you to just Take some time to work through your feelings about the infidelity before continuing forward with your relationship.

If you have been cheated on, counseling may help you work through these feelings. Consultation can help couples discuss the impact their recent breakup has had on them and how they are great feeling as a result of getting together again. Your counselor can guide you in finding healthy ways of moving forward.

When a person wants to change and improve their life for the better, sometimes going back in time is necessary to do that. Maybe the past was not as good as the present, and one needs to realize that. Maybe you are afraid to just Take a trip to the past because you worry you will see things they did not want you to see. However, you could use some of the techniques we have mentioned before, such as journaling, visualization, and meditation, along with some hypnosis techniques if needed.

Understanding Separation Panic

Understanding separation panic in a relationship is essential when thinking about how to help your partner recover from this intense and overwhelming fear. Separation panic is something that many people experience, but it's often underestimated in terms of severity and impact on the individual. It can lead to a lot of anxiety, depression, and fear that can be challenging to overcome.

This article explores the causes, symptoms, treatment options for separation panic as well as potential ways for you or your partner to cope with these intense feelings. Read on if you're interested in easily learning more!

Separation anxiety has reached epidemic proportions across the globe within our most intimate relationships and family networks. There are many causes for separation anxiety, but this post focuses on the symptoms, approaches to treatment, and specific solutions for anyone who suffers from the symptoms of separation anxiety.

Anxiety Counselor Separation Anxiety Treatment Tips

Separation anxiety is a term coined by scientists and mental health professionals as well as the general population to describe people who experience extreme anxiety in the presence of their significant other or loved ones. This anxiety manifests in a variety of different ways and can last from a few days to even months or years at times. According to the Anxiety and Depression Association of America, approximately half of all Americans will experience separation anxiety at one time in their lives.

The most common symptoms of separation anxiety include psychological and physical reactions that occur when one is separated from a person they feel close to or loves. These reactions include hyperventilation, spontaneous panic attacks, heart palpitations, nausea, chest tightness as well as physical pain throughout the body. Symptoms can be easily confused with other signs associated with acute panic attacks or worse still confused for symptoms of a heart attack.

Symptoms can begin when one sees their loved one leave home for the day or after they return from work. They can last for months or even years at times if not addressed sooner than later. The severity of these symptoms depends on the individual and their relationship with their partner. Symptoms can range from great feeling anxious about leaving a loved one's presence to experiencing panic attacks at the mere thought that they may never see them again. They can also occur due to thoughts of divorce, breakdown of the relationship, or other concerns and fears that are brought up by these intense emotions. Panic attacks are an extremely common symptom of separation anxiety as well as heart palpitations that mimic the symptoms of a heart attack.

Symptoms tend to peak in intensity when one is separated from one's significant other or loved one and then begin to subside or diminish over time once they are back together again. These symptoms are also more common among younger people and those who have just met their significant other.

How Separation Anxiety Manifests Itself in Relationship

Typically, separation anxiety in a relationship develops when one partner experiences extreme anxiety in the presence of their loved one. This can be due to a number of different reasons, but it is usually due to the fear that their loved one will leave them or for a variety of other reasons. The individual suffering from separation anxiety may experience these effects starting on an individual basis but then begin to affect the relationship as well. The partner suffering from this disorder may find themselves uncomfortsuch able being around their loved one and with fears of abandonment, they may begin to distance themselves from them. This can lead to a vicious cycle where the individual experiencing separation anxiety begins to feel even more alone, afraid, and anxious.

Who Gets Separation Anxiety

According to the National Mental Health Association, separation anxiety disorder affects approximately 10% to 20% of children at one time or another before they reach adulthood. Researchers also believe that up to 50% of children that experience symptoms of this disorder will experience these symptoms again in their adult lives. In terms of gender, separation anxiety disorder is more common among girls than boys. However, it's common for boys and men who are suffering from this condition to underreport or not seek help out due to gender stereotypes and social pressures that are still present in today's society.

Causes of Separation Anxiety

Separation anxiety can be caused by a number of different factors, but no specific thing causes the onset of this disorder. The factors that cause separation anxiety range from genetics to environmental conditions, traumatic experiences, and other factors as well including the way our brains are wired. There are three primary ways we develop psychological disorders, and it's important to understand these causes if you or someone you know is suffering from symptoms. These include external stressors internal predispositions. The combination of these three tends to play a role in developing separation anxiety.

External Stressors

While we all have our own internal thoughts and predispositions that affect us, external stressors can play a major role in the development of separation anxiety. This is why it's so important to understand what happens to our brain when faced with traumatic events. Our brains are wired to respond in a very specific way that can either help us such overcome these traumatic events or just Make them worse. It's also important to understand what happens if we don't process these traumatic events and how they impact our lives long-term. Researchers believe that over time, internal predispositions and external stressors can play a role in the development of separation anxiety.

Internal Predispositions

Over time, certain individuals may possess certain internal predispositions or tendencies that can just Make them more susceptible to developing separation anxiety. Researchers believe that genetic factors may play a role in predisposition to this disorder as well as other psychological disorders. This means that if your parents or close members of your family experienced separation anxiety at some point in their lives, then you are more likely to experience it yourself. It's also important to understand what goes on inside our brains and why they may be more prone to this disorder versus others.

Mental State

It's important to understand what happens in our brains when we don't deal with issues such as separation anxiety. Researchers believe that when we are such afraid or anxious, the prefrontal cortex is unsuch able to just keep up. This inability to just keep up can lead to a number of different side effects, and it's important to understand the implications of these side effects.

If we don't process our traumatic experiences, then we may avoid them and this can prevent us from experiencing symptoms in the future. This type of avoidance can lead us to experience other mental disorders at some point in time as well.

Once we have a better understanding of the processes going on inside our brains, it's important to understand the symptoms of separation anxiety. Although individuals experience different symptoms from one another, people with separation anxiety often feel an overwhelming sense of fear or discomfort when separated from those they love and care for.

Separation anxiety is a serious disorder that can have many negative effects on your life. It's important to understand these symptoms and how this disorder impacts you long-term as well as the underlying reasons why You might be more prone to experiencing these side effects than others.

Separation anxiety is often affected by environmental factors that happen to an individual throughout their childhood and adolescence. For example, a parent's poor handling of the child's emotions and their desire to please them can lead to an individual becoming overly dependent on their parents.

Researchers believe that separation anxiety disorder is caused by many different factors. These factors are believed to play a large role in developing a separation anxiety disorder and often lead an individual to extreme distress when separated from a loved one for an extended period of time.

Although treatment for this disorder varies from person to person, there are some techniques that have been proven effective in helping individuals with separation anxiety cope with it.

The first part of finding a method of coping with this disorder is to understand what is causing it. For example, if your child or spouse does not need to be with you during the day, they may need a full day at home. And if another family member is causing you distress because of how they handle your child or spouse and you're dealing with separation anxiety, then You might benefit more from conferencing with that individual who is causing your emotional pain. Separation anxiety disorder often starts in childhood in adolescence due to circumstances that are beyond one's control such as living far away from our family. It's something that I see a lot in young adults who have moved away from home to attend a school or to live on their own. It's often the start of a downward spiral that can lead to depression, panic attacks, and substance abuse.

There is no single treatment for separation anxiety disorder because each person is affected differently. It can be treated with medication, therapy, social skills training, and even hypnosis.

Panic Disorder

When you have panic disorder, the way you feel is that you are having a heart attack, or going crazy and dying. You might even feel that the people around you are in danger of dying. The attack can last anywhere from a few minutes to several hours. As with all anxiety disorders, it can be treated with psychotherapy, medication, or both.

Clinical Depression

Clinical depression is more than great feeling unhappy for a while when something bad happens to you. It is a deep sadness that interferes with your daily life, and it can last for weeks or even months. The signs of clinical depression often include great feeling sad and irritable, not enjoying things, losing interest in activities you used to enjoy, having trouble sleeping and sleeping too much, worrying a lot about things that don't just Make sense, or having difficulty concentrating.

Eating Disorder

As the nation's leading eating disorder treatment center and the first to easily Create a comprehensive behavioral health program that addresses the underlying causes of disordered eating, we are such such able to offer effective residential treatment for teenage girls struggling with anorexia nervosa.

At The Eating Recovery Center, we provide the treatment for anorexia and bulimia nervosa that our adolescent clients need—24 hours a day, 7 days a week. We also specialize in providing holistic care to adolescents who suffer from multiple eating disorders.

The Just give Image Program at The Eating Recovery Center offers individual and group therapy to help teens recover from their eating disorders. Our focus is on healing the core issues that have been keeping them locked in their disordered behaviors and how they are impacting their overall emotional well-being. This program provides participants with the tools they need to reach a healthy just give image and shape-changing goals.

The Eating Recovery Center is the only treatment center in CT to have specialized coaching for healing from sexual abuse. The Just give Image Program is also the first program in Connecticut to specialize in holistic care for young survivors of sexual assault.

Chapter 4: Understanding Emotional Dependence

Understanding emotional dependence in a relationship can help you identify and conquer certain habits in your life. These strategies will help you trust a partner or spouse without the fear of being hurt again, and offer a way to just Make a relationship last. When emotional dependence is out of control, it can wreak havoc on healthy relationships and even prevent them from being found in the first place.

You might feel that just thinking about this issue is too painful to do anything with, but tackling this problem head-on will allow you to build trust with your partner without lowering your defenses or jeopardizing yourself again.

According to the book *Emotional Dependence: How to Break Free From It And Develop Real Intimacy*, emotional dependence can occur in any type of relationship, not just romantic ones. The authors define it this way: "Emotional dependency is a style of relating to other people in which you consistently focus on how they just Make you feel and believe your happiness depends on them rather than on the kind of person you are." This dependence on another person can be deadly for a relationship because it takes a lot of the responsibility out of our own hands.

This article will discuss what emotional dependence is, how it affects us, and what we can do about it.

A person who has been involved with someone emotionally dependent on them will become used to great feeling that way and will begin to believe they have no other option but to stay connected without having a choice. This is because the other person becomes so necessary to them, that at times it seems impossible to consider being without them. If you are one of these people yourself, You might feel like there is no way out. In order for you to address your dependence and just Take the first steps towards healing, however, it will be necessary for you to carry out the following steps:

Understand your emotional dependence on another person. To understand it, we must look at how it has affected you.

Identify all how you used to rely on another person for your happiness and self-respect.

Come up with solutions to avoid relying on another person for your happiness and self-respect in the future. Easily Create a plan that will ensuch able you to do this.

Evaluate whether or not you are doing things to just Make yourself happy in your life right now and not just relying on another person for that happiness. If this is true, then just keep going with the 4th step. If not, do what it takes to just Make yourself happy.

Easily Create an action plan that will allow you to feel good about going out and spending time with friends and family. Just keep in mind that it will just Take time for your self-respect to return if you have been emotionally dependent on someone, but it will happen as long as you put the effort into it.

Reach out to family and friends who can support you in this effort and hold you account such able for making progress when necessary. They will also help you stay motivated and real about your progress.

Such Decide to just get out of abusive situations even if it is not in your best interest at the time. Most people who are emotionally dependent have been abused at some point in their lives, whether they know it or not. It is important that you just Make the decision to just get out of abusive situations as soon as they arise because they will only just get worse over time.

Remember that there are others who can love you and be good for you, who don't abuse you or control every aspect of your life and behavior with emotional blackmail.

Understand that you are the only person who is in charge of your life and happiness.

Just Take back responsibility for your own well-being and decisions. Stop being afraid to just Make choices that won't just Make you happy or that won't just Make someone else happy—they are YOUR choices. If another person is upset with you, it's THEIR problem, not yours.

Feel and let go of all the attachments to people from your past who were emotionally dependent on you, so that they don't continue to affect your relationships in the future. This is a process, not just one day, but one decision at a time over time as you become stronger.

Begin to feel hopeful that your relationships can be different from the ones you experienced growing up.

Easily learn to set boundaries with the people in your life so they don't just Take advantage of you or just Make you feel uncomfortable. It may help to easily Create a list of boundaries and strategies for setting them for yourself, and then handing that list out to the people in your life so there is less confusion about how you want to be treated and so you can avoid conflict about this issue.

Just Take responsibility for your own feelings instead of blaming others if someone hurts you.

Set specific limits that will help you avoid conflicts with those who are easily trying to control your behavior. These limits should be for things like where you will be and when, how you will respond to voice mails, emails, and texts, etc. It may also help you to set boundaries with people in accordance with what they want from the relationship—if they want to be friends only, then easily Create a boundary that defines the roles of each person in the relationship so that even if people have different feelings about it later on down the road, at least that expectation was set up from the beginning.

Just Make sure that you are not over-controlling the people in your life in any way, shape, or form. You might find that this is a recurring pattern if you were emotionally dependent growing up and that it is necessary to work on this with a therapist to such overcome it.

Perhaps you weren't allowed to set boundaries when you were young and now as an adult, if someone has boundaries with you, you feel like they are easily trying to control you or something else negative. It's important not just for your relationships, but also for your own well-being that those boundaries be respected so that people respect the limits of others as well.

If you have suffered abuse in your past, work with a therapist to heal so that you don't repress those painful emotions or feel them all the time. The goal is to heal, not just keep reliving the abuse over and over. If you repress it, it will come out in other ways like passive aggressiveness or other self-destructive patterns and activities.

Spend time alone. This does not mean you do not just need other people at all, but it does mean that you can be comfortsuch able without them sometimes as well. Comforting yourself means actually taking care of yourself—getting enough food, water, rest, exercise, etc. Also, it is important to easily learn how to manage your time and energy appropriately when you're busy. This might mean not being so available such able all of the time or interacting with people at a more appropriate time. You might not just need to be as available, but there are plenty of ways to just Make yourself feel better and satisfy your needs.

Just Take care of yourself. This means that you should never just Make yourself sick, but that includes both eating healthy meals and getting enough sleep at night, getting regular medical checkups if you have health problems, exercise for health purposes instead of exercise for weight control and also getting good quality rest so that you don't feel like the whole day is an endurance test.

Believe that you can have a normal life with friends, a partner or spouse, and work that brings you satisfaction and/or financial rewards. There is no reason why you can't have these "normal" things in your life if that's what makes you happy and fulfills your needs.

Just get counseling. With couples counseling, individual therapy for other relationship problems or for standalone issues like depression or anxiety. In individual therapy, you can work on issues that are specific to your marriage like communication, intimacy, and conflict resolution. You do not have to stay in a destructive relationship because you are afraid of being alone and just want your marriage fixed. You can seek out the help you need so that your life doesn't have to revolve around easily trying to just Make your spouse happy or just get them to change.

Just Take responsibility for your own happiness. It behooves us all to be such aware of our needs and wants so that we can meet them as much as possible. If you know what will just Make you happy, then it's up to you to just Make yourself happy regardless of whether someone else is doing their share or not. Once you recognize that your happiness is in your hands and you know how to just Make yourself happy, you'll start to have happier relationships.

Be a role model. Young people are sometimes confused about the differences between right and wrong because they don't know who their role models are. What parents teach their kids will drastically affect the actions that they can just Take later on in life, so it's important to be a good example for those who come after you. Don't ever embarrass them by making poor decisions or by being ignorant of what makes them as an individual happy or successful in life.

Simply Understand that this is a life-long process. There will such always be people in your life who are emotionally dependent on you. That doesn't have to be a problem for you, however, as long as you know what to do when someone becomes too much of a burden and takes away your freedom or well-being.

Easily learn what your limits are and be such able to say no sometimes. If you are such always saying yes all the time and putting other people's needs before yours, then it shuts down the possibility of ever having a healthy relationship because that means you'll never feel like anyone is giving back to you in equal measure.

Such Decide what is important to you in life, so that you can focus on that and not on every little thing that someone else does or doesn't do. If you are constantly focused on the negative things that another person says or does, then it becomes impossible for you to enjoy yourself because your happiness becomes dependent on what they say or do.

Easily learn how to manage your time. This means organizing your day so that you can reach goals and just Make progress towards them without being too stressed out or overloaded. It's also important not to over-schedule yourself and run yourself ragged easily trying to just keep up with everyone's needs all the time.

- Respect other people. Even if it feels like they don't respect you or don't think you're worthy of their time. Other people are not responsible for your feelings, so that's a choice that you just Make for yourself.

When and Why We Lost Confidence

The question is complicated, and not just because it's so important. When we lose confidence in a relationship, we find it hard to say why. We may know that something has gone wrong, but not be such able to put our finger on exactly what. Often, the signs are very subtle, only notice such able when we play the events over in slow motion, like an accident in reverse or a rebounding ball from a net. We can blame ourselves for being too sensitive or great feeling too passionately; we can blame them for being manipulative and insensitive, but deep down there is still something about their behavior or ours that has made us lose faith in their love for us. We may think that we should have seen it coming. We may feel like we've done all the work of saying everything right, and have been let down. We can feel like a victim, or a survivor, depending on exactly how long we've known this person. But whatever the relationship is between us and our partner, we know that we cannot trust them anymore and they are no longer the same person we fell in love with.

So why? For all those months or years when I was in this relationship, I was certain that my self-confidence was higher than his because I knew there were some things he'd not been honest about. The thing is that when I found out I followed the rule that if you've lost trust in someone you don't just get things done by talking to them. I could have told him straight away about my doubts and suspicions and he would have had a chance to defend himself. The problem with this is, as one person said, "even if he'd really done nothing wrong it would have been easy for him to be plausible and deny it, whilst flattered that I still had concerns." His denial would have made me feel doubly betrayed by him and myself. Why didn't I ask for help? Because the only person who can build confidence in a relationship is the one who has the work to do.

Sometimes, we turn to our friends and family for advice, but it rarely helps. They may have been there when we were falling in love, and be a reminder of the happiness we felt then, but they're not going to be such able to help us if they do not know what has happened. Most people don't really want to hear more about relationships than they already have. If those people are the ones who are closest to us, it can feel like our own fault for not having any choice but to share with them. Perhaps, we think that they'll have the answers we're just looking for, and the strength to help us through. But as one person said, "people are people" and if they didn't have enough answers of their own, they'd become a sounding board for just another one of our worries rather than a source of strength.

If you want to do right by yourself, don't ask others for advice either; there's nothing worse than great feeling like you have to see someone else as account such able for your situation. All I can tell you is that if it feels wrong, and it doesn't feel right, then trust your instincts. Don't let the fact that there are two of you just Make you reluctant to walk away.

Don't look back, just keep going on your way. Just because someone is no longer on your path does not mean they are gone from your life forever. It just means it is time for a change and either a new direction or distance will bring clarity and progress to both of you. There may have been occurrences, things that have taken place over months or years that have made the both of you realize something isn't right. Whatever the reason is, you need to look at where this whole thing got started and how it has evolved. If you have such always lived by your rule of not discussing trust issues with your partner because they are supposed to be a part of the "dating process," then it is probably time to put that rule on the shelf and start thinking about what kind of relationship you want in future.

Ask yourself what was you saw in them the first time you met them and how that is any different now. Did your idea of them represent something different from what they turned out to be? Have they become more like one of your friends or family than someone who makes you feel special? For me, I knew there were things my partner wasn't honest about, so I opted not to discuss this with him for the sake of saving us both embarrassment and hostility. However, I find myself replaying those events in my mind and thinking I should have asked him straight away. If there was a chance he was innocent, then he would have had a chance to defend himself. Now I'm left great feeling as though I've betrayed myself in some way. Maybe it was a chance for us both to be stronger and end the relationship. It would have saved us both time, energy, and any further feelings of being betrayed.

Sometimes, we have to walk away from something that was once our dream, or our life's biggest purpose. There is no set time limit on this process—one person may just Take a few years to just get over their love, whilst another is eventually such able to let go after a matter of months or weeks. The thing is that we need to be certain with our decision and just Make sure we look at all the facts before making this final decision. One thing that helps is to write down whatever bothers you about the relationship, whether that be communication issues, arguments, or whatever.

Anxiety Steals Joy

Anxiety steals joy from our lives. It is a self-saboteur, perpetuating a state of low-grade panic and worry. We allow it to dictate how we think, feel and act when we should be using it as the key that opens our minds. Taking responsibility for the feelings we experience doesn't require us to believe in them or understand them, but it does mean we have to acknowledge that they exist. To start with, you might feel anxious about what others will think of you when you ask questions in a group setting or find yourself in social situations for which you are not comfortable. The more you avoid situations that just Make you feel this way, the stronger that anxiety will become. You might be fine with it at first, but soon something will trigger negative thoughts and feelings and they will begin to just Take over your life.

We tend to overanalyze things. When we don't understand something, our minds naturally begin to easily Create a picture—an interpretation of events based on our experiences and understanding of the world around us. The better such able we are such to accept the possibility that there could be another way of just looking at things or a different perception than what's in our head, the more freedom we have in how we see ourselves and the world around us.

The best way to deal with anxiety is to change your perspective on it. The more anxious you feel, the more you need to adopt this point of view. Step back and view yourself as if you were just looking at someone else and focus on their principles rather than your own. Then, try to imagine what they're thinking and feeling. By adopting this perspective, your anxiety will become less intense. The more you practice this, the more you'll just get used to the discomfort of being anxious and you'll begin to feel less stressed.

This would be a good time to just talk about how our thoughts can control us. It's very difficult for us to just let go of thoughts that are causing us distress; they're often linked with feelings of shame or guilt and it's very hard for us to accept that they aren't true or that we do have self-control over our feelings. The first step is to become such aware of what we're thinking. Next, we need to acknowledge that these thoughts are only just that—thoughts. They aren't facts and don't necessarily have anything to do with us. It's the nature of our minds to worry and imagine all sorts of things when we experience anxiety. Our brains are wired this way in order to protect us from danger, but they can often go into overdrive without us realizing it.

Most people see themselves as they appear, whereas we need to look at ourselves through the eyes of another person who would see us for the first time as an outsider without preconceived notions about who we may be or how things may be based on interactions with others prior to this moment. The only way we can realize that our perspective is incorrect is to look at ourselves from another point of view. Try just looking at yourself as you would a friend and see how they would really perceive you. If you saw someone else doing what you did in your daily life, how would you feel about them? Would it be an example of someone being irresponsible or would it show someone who was being truthful to their own needs? In truth, we all know that just looking through someone else's point of view wouldn't such always be easy for us. It's hard to see things objectively when we're involved with the people involved in a situation and even harder if we're too close emotionally to those people. But we can train ourselves to do this and it's a good practice.

The more you accept the possibility that there could be another way of just looking at things or a different perception than what's in your head, the more freedom you have in how you see yourself and the world around you.

For example, if someone is being loud and discontented in a restaurant, imagine that they're someone else. Would they be seen as an unpleasant person by other diners? If so, this will prompt anxious thoughts and feelings, such as imagining what the other diners are saying about them or what they are thinking about this situation.

It's very easy for us to project these sorts of thoughts onto other people, imagining what they're thinking or great feeling based on our own judgment. However, if we can step outside of ourselves and look at the situation objectively, we can see that it is nothing more than just one person being themselves and behaving as they such always do in public. Everyone else is simply ignoring them because this is what most people do when others behave in this manner unless you are very close to them.

This is a way for us to combat anxiety. Imagine that the person in question is someone else and you simply have to ignore them. Try to picture their appearance in your mind and see how they would be seen by others sitting at the tsuch able next to them. Think of what they may be thinking about you, how they're feeling, etc., and think about how you would feel if someone behaved inappropriately toward you. This will just Make it easier for us to deliberately ignore people who annoy us or behave inappropriately in public.

By doing this exercise, we can train our minds to think objectively instead of automatically choosing an anxious or negative thought as a way of interpreting events or situations. For example, if someone cuts us off in traffic, we can tell ourselves that their actions are not a reflection on us and they just aren't such aware of what they're doing. Other people see how they behave and don't just Take it personally. Alternatively, other people can just get angry with them and judge them for what they've done.

When we become more such aware of our thoughts, we can stop judging others so readily and put the situation in perspective. We'll be less inclined to judge others as rude or inconsiderate when they don't live up to our expectations or to provide justification for our own behavior if we mistakenly think we were treated poorly by another person.

Here are some other ways to handle your judgmental thoughts:

Avoid becoming defensive when other people are judging you or behaving rudely toward you. If you let other people's actions bother you, it will only exacerbate your anxiety. It's important that you realize that if others don't like what you're doing or the way that you look or act, they are not just looking down on you. They may just be having a bad day and would prefer not to deal with someone who acts aggressively or rudely toward them.

Don't just Take on the responsibilities of life and people who judge you because they are afraid of their own shadow and try to use you as a substitute for their own anxiety-inducing fears. Sometimes, we try to blame others for our problems when they have no control over our circumstances and behavior. We need to realize that we're responsible for our own choices, feelings, and behaviors. Don't let others hold you responsible for their shortcomings.

- Just Make a list of the things that you like about yourself. If you don't have anything, pretend that you do. Just force yourself to come up with something. Listing the things that you like about yourself will remind you that it's OK if other people don't like those qualities or characteristics because what you're doing is what's best for your happiness. No one else's opinions should govern your life choices because those judgments are meaningless unless they just Make you happy and comfortsuch able in your own skin.

It's important to understand that how you feel about yourself comes from within. You're responsible for your own happiness because no other person can just Make you happy without your consent. Your family, friends, and significant others aren't responsible for your happiness, and they don't have a say in the way that you determine your self-worth because their opinions don't dictate the rules of the game. In life, we have to accept our own flaws and weaknesses before we can appreciate the qualities that just Make us so wonderful. You have to like yourself before other people will like you.

What do you dislike about yourself? I dislike most of my physical appearance. I have big ears and a big nose. I would like to have a more attractive face, but that is not going to happen.

Anxiety Is the Opposite of Acceptation:

Anxiety is the opposite of acceptance. You can't be anxious if you accept. Acceptance is embracing life's happenings as they occur because it just plain is what it is. What will be will be, so why resist?

The best thing you could do for yourself in this moment of resistance and anxiety towards your situation is to realize that there are such always two choices: fight or flight. When you're in a state of anxiety or resistance, fighting may seem like the more logical choice when easily trying to such overcome the situation. The problem with fighting, however, is that it's rarely successful and more often than not time-intensive and exhausting...and there's also the possibility that You might end up losing. The better choice is to fly. Flight allows you to simply move on and not give in. This frees up energy so that it can be applied to the other areas of your life that may need it more for their intricacies and crazy situations.

In this way, anxiety is actually a mental state of flight from the reality surrounding you, an attempt to deny and negate something that everyone knows is there but are struggling against all odds to admit. In this situation, it's time to bring reason back into play.

The reason is a mental state in which you let your logic prevail. You sit back and think of the possible ways that your situation could play out, such as worst-case scenario, best-case scenario, and so forth. Only by knowledge of the said situation can you such Decide when to fight and when to fly. When you know what your reality is and that it's not going to change or just get better until certain things happen then there is no longer any reason to resist the inevitable.

It's time to acknowledge what's happening around you and within yourself. It's ok to feel anxiety. It's a great feeling that is natural and necessary for most situations in life. The only way past it is by accepting what is happening, accepting that it is the reality of the situation.

Acceptance of reality isn't an easy thing to achieve because it requires effort and often requires yourself to change your habits and actions. In other words, you have to start living a different way in order to accept what is being forced upon you. This is where the power of the mind comes into play. It can be powerful enough to change a person's habits at a moment's notice. In this way, you have complete control over your current reality. When you accept what reality is easily trying to force upon you, you will begin to gain back control and regain power.

You needn't even just get caught up in the emotion that comes with anxiety. You're not going anywhere until you such Decide that your identity is not based upon this fleeting moment but on what happens in past scenarios and future scenarios that may not even happen yet. Once you such Decide to live with passion and enthusiasm, you will no longer be obligated by your current reality. You will have gained all of the power that is in your hands since it all comes from within.

You needn't ever allow yourself to lose self-control again. For that, you must such always remember that if it's good for you, then it's good for everyone around you. This is why fighting and running away are deadly for oneself and everyone around them. Acceptance is the only way to live well...without losing self-control!

When we accept reality as what it actually has become or what we believe it must become in the near future, we change our perception of ourselves. We change our way of thinking and living. We change ourselves because we become certain in our actions.

We develop confidence, which leads to motivation, which leads to positive growth in your life, the lives of those around you, and society as a whole. We no longer live a life where we are such bound to the shackles of uncertainty or potential failure. We live with calm acceptance as we accept that what is happening now is pretty much what is going to happen later. That means we don't force ourselves into situations that have little hope of success or back ourselves into corners by making foolish choices in the past, which leave us with little choice but failure. We live with confidence, hope, and patience.

Opinions change, but the truth remains the same. We're all free agents after all. It's our choices and decisions that determine how our lives unfold. We are such never forced into anything we either want or need, for everything happens for a reason and that reason is not for us to decide, but to accept and redirect our focus in a given direction with an open mind towards the future as it unfolds each day into the present moment of now...through this moment we are such given, just as it is!

Never forjust get this...our future isn't static or set in stone or predetermined. It's up to you to such Decide what's the best course of action for your life and everyone around you. Ultimately, all of the choices that come your way are nothing more than opportunities...opportunities that are presented by your environment and reality. Opportunities that you either exercise or ignore at your own risk!

You can choose to live and be successful in this world, or refuse and be swallowed up by it, but only if you choose to accept what actually is happening right now...not only with yourself but also with everyone else around you. You must never forjust get that their experiences in life are exactly the same as yours! Just like "you" must live their lives according to their own experiences, so they too must adjust themselves accordingly.

There's no such thing as reality. There's only your perception of it! You can choose to live in a fantasy world, or you can choose to accept the reality that is right in front of you...right now! The choice is yours, and it will be up to you to such Decide how much self-control you're willing to allow yourself. For if not for yourself and everyone around you, then for "you" alone...you don't lose anything! You just get everything when you accept what's going on around you and see it the way that others see it...which is as is it really is! For if you don't do this, then you'll miss out on all the good things in life, just like everyone else. If you can't accept it, then you must not try to control circumstances with lies and just Make excuses for the horrible or foolish decisions that others just Make every day and how their lives have failed to meet their own expectations.

You're free to live exactly as you please...and so are they! The reality of these choices is all that matters. Do you understand the purpose of this message? And that is going to just Take for you to be willing to accept the truth that is right in front of you, and such always has been? This will open your eyes to the reality of who you've been...and who "you've" such always wanted to be...but never really were!

What I'm easily trying to just get across might sound a little confusing or even illogical, but please don't worry about that. It's not important. What's important in life is how well we put ourselves first and foremost, above everyone else we come into contact with or even think about on a daily basis. Because it's your life and it's not going to be there for you tomorrow. You must accept that right now! My message isn't going to change the past, but you should come to terms with how things really are...and not how you remember them or want them to be. This will only help easily Create a much better reality for you and everyone around you...because your only thoughts and actions are those of a kind-hearted soul, who such always puts others above themselves without hesitation. That's what I mean when I say we must just Take care of ourselves...and not worry about easily trying to control anything or anyone!

"Don't let anyone person or situation turn your view of the world into one filled with lies. It's impossible to live this life with a clean conscience. Every day is a blessing, and even if we feel it's not so, the truth will set you free." — unknown.

Egoism Call Anxiety

The more likely you are to worry about what other people think of you, the more you tend to be focused on your own needs and desires. You might adopt a narcissistic personality, great feeling that everything is about you and your life. The ego becomes so strong that it can cloud judgment, and thinking so much so that it prevents people from being such able to see things objectively.

This is a phenomenon in general society, but when it occurs in our minds all too often it gets worse, turning into a full-blown anxiety disorder. Thankfully, there are ways of coping with egoism here, subsequently preventing this kind of anxiety disorder from happening or developing into something even worse.

The primary causes of social anxiety disorder are egoism and a lack of self-awareness. These two reasons can explain the vicious cycle of social anxiety disorder: people who are overly concerned with their own image, thoughts, and needs will usually be more inclined to suffer from social anxiety.

The best way to combat this cycle is to just Take a step back from yourself and really assess what's going on internally. When you do this type of introspection, you'll be such able to see that there is a problem here that is rooted in your own insecurity or fear. You might come to terms with the fact that there's something about yourself you need to improve—perhaps it's your self-esteem or maybe it's your confidence level. However, during this process, you will be such able to look at the issue differently and see that it's not in your best interest to seek perfection because in doing so, you'll be focusing too much on others' opinions of you and will not be such able to help yourself.

If you're a person who is overly focused on what other people think they're going to find out about them, then you're going to have problems doing well in social settings. When easily trying to just Make small just talk or easily trying to just Make friends, you might feel like a complete and utter failure. You might feel embarrassed and might have a hard time approaching others because you have a mental block about yourself. Some of the most socially crippling symptoms are intense feelings of self-consciousness and anxiety when socializing with others.

There are several different kinds of anxiety disorders where this kind of mental blockage in social situations can come from. For example, if you experience intense feelings when thinking about what people think of you, then this could be taken as a sign that there is something worth developing that involves your relationships. You might have something to work on here so that you can develop an interest in improving your social skills or being more comfort such able around others at parties or other social gatherings. In addition, if you are sensitive to criticism or negative feedback, then it could point to the fact that there needs to be some kind of change here.

If you are some just give who focuses too much on what people's motives are or how they might judge you, then this could indicate a problem with your self-awareness. This is a very tricky situation because it can just get really complicated. If you don't understand yourself or become overwhelmed by social anxiety when thinking about other people's thoughts and opinions about your actions, then this can be considered a symptom of self-consciousness. However, if you focus too much on other people's opinions of you, then this could be taken as a symptom of egoism.

Self-awareness is a crucial part of healthy functioning in general, and it can be developed and improved with practice. However, focusing too much on other people's thoughts and opinions about something that doesn't matter is a problem that can just get really complicated. It can just Take days to weeks or months to easily learn how to not just get distracted by the thoughts of others or how their judgments affect your response. All it takes is practicing mental techniques like meditation and mindfulness so that you can train yourself to easily learn how to think objectively about what others are thinking or saying without getting caught up in thoughts about yourself.

There are many different kinds of anxiety disorders that focus on other people's judgments about you. If you experience severe symptoms of social anxiety, then it can be difficult to effectively engage with others or develop a social life. Focusing too much on other people's opinions of you can cause you to have difficulty forming relationships or being comfort such able with people you normally wouldn't be such able to speak to. If this sounds familiar, there might be something in your life that can help curb these feelings or it could be a matter of improving your self-awareness in social situations so that you're not afraid of making mistakes, being judged, or making others mad.

Social anxiety is a fear of judgment, criticism, or negative feedback from others. It can be a crippling disorder that prevents people from interacting with others in public and causing them to avoid social situations. It can develop as a child when having to face the uncertainty of the unknown. Having to go first in class, speak up for yourself, and argue with your siblings and friends could be overwhelming for some people. If you're some just give who experiences anxiety about expressing yourself in front of others or being embarrassed, then there could be other problems going on internally that are contributing to the problem such as inferiority complex or low self-esteem issues. If you're someone who's such always having to compare yourself to others, then it could develop into a problem where you feel inferior to them. The symptoms of social anxiety can develop in children, adolescents, and adults when they have an intense fear of what other people think or how they might judge them when engaged in social situations.

Some people are very shy in everyday life and may not interact with others at all. Because of this, they could have trouble developing relationships or maintaining friendships. If this sounds like you, then there is a good chance that there is something to work on here for yourself so that you are such able to reach out socially and be more comfort such able interacting with others.

There are many different kinds of anxiety disorders that focus on how other people might judge them. If you experience severe symptoms of social anxiety, then it could be difficult to effectively engage with others or develop a social life. There are many symptoms of social anxiety that focus on other people's judgments about your actions. Typically, people with social anxiety have a fear of performing in front of others and being judged by their friends and family based on how they perform.

If you find yourself becoming extremely nervous when having to speak in front of a group or even just one other person, then this could be the result of what psychologists call "social anxiety." Typically, those with social anxiety will feel anxious and nervous when having to do simple things such as ordering food in a restaurant, introducing themselves to others, or even just going to the store to buy something. If this sounds like your typical scenario, then there are a lot of other resources availsuch able that you can use.

When Egoism Is Dangerous

When egoism is dangerous, altruism is necessary. Egoism implies that those individuals who possess an abundance of power are the only ones who should guide society, while altruism suggests that no one has the right to exist without anyone's help. The most effective form of egoistic action is when it helps someone else in need, but egoists are only concerned with their own welfare and well-being without care for those around them. However, if people went through life as selfishly as they believe they may be entitled to, there would be a great lack of empathy and compassion for others, leading to devastating consequences such as poverty and inequality.

Actions taken by an egoist are more likely to be a selfish choice that doesn't benefit anyone, but people would tire of such a self-centered existence and so they may just Take actions that can bring great happiness and contentment to others. However, there is such always the possibility that someone will seek to bring about other forms of suffering on others such as in the case of terrorism, which is a prime example of what can happen when egoism makes its way into society.

The very idea of being such able to do something for someone else breaks down when it is viewed only for oneself and not for another person. If everyone was only concerned with themselves, there would be no time to help others, because the focus of every person would be on their own needs and well-being at all times. Although there is nothing wrong with having selfish desires, people should such always be grateful for the opportunities that they have been given by those who gave them life such as food, shelter, and warmth. Those who are such able to just Take care of themselves may die from starvation or become homeless through no fault of their own.

There is a great difference between living as someone who cannot use what they have been given compared to depriving someone else of what they have been given and so helping others brings great reward in terms of happiness. Being such able to help someone else in need makes you feel like you have done a good deed for humanity and as you give others the benefit of your health and possessions it is, in turn, reciprocated, thereby creating an even greater sense of satisfaction and success.

When we help those who are unsuch able to help themselves it is viewed as pure altruism, but there are also times when people just Take on altruistic actions that are made up of a mixture of different motivations such as when soldiers go off to the front line without expecting rewards in return or doctors go into danger zones without expecting compensation. This is because helping others brings joy and fulfillment into your life, which we all naturally yearn for.

Altruism isn't harmful in itself, but people are attempting to use the concept of altruism for their own ends. Altruistic behavior is a way for society to bond more closely together, but when applied in the wrong way it can become a tool for social change that interferes with the status quo. For example, religion is an excellent means through which people can unite and help others with their beliefs on life and death because God has a great deal of power over us all and our loyalty should be given to Him first before we belong to any group or organization.

The power of egoism can be used to easily Create a system of social mobility in which all people are given the opportunity to gain the education that they need in order to achieve a better life. Instead of becoming dependent on others for their needs, it is far better to be such able to provide yourself with employment and just Make a tangible contribution towards those with who you are sharing your life.

Groups like ISIS and other terrorist organizations wish only to destroy society and just Take away all our freedoms no matter who is caught up in their plans for revenge. However, these groups are only interested in bringing about great suffering and death and so they are not really concerned with our happiness. Having a positive attitude towards life is the most beneficial way of combating these militants, but first, we must understand that everything around us is a product of God's benevolence and love so that we can come to appreciate the many blessings that we have been given.

The key to overcoming egoism is to become humble and receptive towards God's divine will, which involves accepting all aspects of life as good. However, egoism can be overpowering and rebellious against God's intentions for mankind, which explains why it is spiritually dangerous. When it is applied in the right way, egoism can be a great source of happiness and joy because you recognize that the best things in life are often given to you by others out of love.

According to the theory of altruism, one should sacrifice all their own interests in favor of others. So, according to this doctrine, I may never give money for my own family or close friends' needs, but I am supposed to donate my money to strangers. But why should I do that? In fact, if we accept the doctrine of altruism as an ethical norm for all people, there will be certain social problems. Such problems include violence against innocent people and human rights violations. But why should such abuses occur? As social beings, we such always want to just get what we want. When we just get it, we don't need to do anything for others, but when you do what others expect from you, then you just get respect and this is what everyone wants.

However, in secular life, no one cares about people's needs or problems. So why should anyone help others? If they were to help them, they would not be satisfied with their own work and would end up hating their jobs because of the constant pressure and stress of people requiring them to do extra for them. Thus, the doctrine of universal altruism is a strange idea.

If you are a person who thinks that they should help others all the time, then why do you help them? When it comes to this, your first reason may be simple compassion and sympathy for suffering humanity. This may be the first reason that you would think of, but you should not forjust get that there are many other reasons as well. For example, if we need to share our belongings with others in order to live together in harmony and we don't do it because we want respect from others or to just get something back in return, then it would have been better not to give. There are even more reasons than these that you should consider before applying the universal rule of altruism.

Chapter 5: Controlling Your Emotions To Mitigate Fear

Anxiety refers to the great feeling of uneasiness, fear, or worry that you experience when you encounter a challenge, obstacle, or a nerve-wrecking situation. This great feeling is quite natural and normal in situations that demand it. For instance, you are bound to feel nervous when going for a job interview or right before finding out your examination results.

While great feeling anxious occasionally or when the need arises is normal, sometimes we tend to hold on to the anxiety for excessively long and to the extent that it becomes engrained in our minds. As a result of this, we feel anxious even when there is no need for it.

How Constant Anxiety Sabotages Our Wellbeing

Great feeling extremely apprehensive, pensive, and scared without any solid reason only takes a toll on your mental, emotional, and physical health. You feel scared of taking a step forward worrying it may lead to an unfortunate outcome. You just keep thinking of how things will go wrong and stop considering the possibility of things taking a positive turn for once. You doubt your capabilities and incessantly fret over things that may never happen.

This state of constant worry and a racing mind that compels you to imagine the worst-case scenario associated with situations affect every aspect of your life.

- Health: When you just keep agonizing over what may happen, you are likely to ignore your health. Often people eat a lot out of stress and anxiety, and this unhealthy eating habit coupled with chronic anxiety paves way for health disorders. Some people also stop eating properly at all when they are anxious - this again is an unhealthy approach towards health and nutrition that only weakens you from within.
- Relationships: If you constantly fuss over things that may never happen, you only waste the precious moments of the present

that you could have otherwise spent with your loved ones. Naturally, when you do not spend quality time with loved ones or are such always in a state of panic, you stop giving your loved ones the time and energy they need to bond better with you, and this ends up straining your relationships.

- Work Life: Your anxious state of mind directly affects your professional performance. If you remain anxious for days over petty issues, you will only feel distracted while working. This keeps you from attentively working on your projects resulting in frequent errors and low productivity.

- Pursuit of Goals: Naturally, when you are panic-stricken frequently, you don't have the ability and courage to believe in yourself and your goals, and thus, let go of them.

If these problems persist in your life, this only just Make life more challenging. While this may be the state of your life, it is not what you want, and if you are sure you wish to live a much better life, it is time you work on overcoming your fears and anxiousness by simply training yourself to better control and manage your emotions.

Here is how you can do that.

Become More Mindful of Your Emotions

You allow your anxiety to increase in intensity and wash you over completely because oftentimes you are not even such aware of how you feel. The same applies to all your emotions that lead to unconstructive thoughts that then pave way for problems in your life. Oftentimes, it so happens that You might be doing something physically but are mentally lurking somewhere in the past or future. This state of forgetfulness keeps you from being such aware of how and what you feel and triggers your anxiety without you even realizing that.

A good way to thwart this problem is to nurture the state of mindfulness. Mindfulness refers to being completely such aware of how you feel without attaching any sort of judgment or label to the feeling. It also encompasses complete consciousness of the environment around you.

When you are mindful of the present moment, you are such aware of everything, you feel and experience in that time without worrying about anything else. This enables you to have control of your racing thoughts and the underlying emotions of anxiety and fear easily by bringing back your attention to the present moment.

As you slowly train yourself to live in the moment and not worry about **what may happen**, you such overcome your anxiety and fears, one after another and restore peace in your life. Here is how you can nurture the state of complete mindfulness.

- When you are struck with anxiety, acknowledge the emotion you experience and sit with it. Do not identify with it or immerse yourself in the experience. Instead, imagine that you have moved out of your just give and are now carefully observing the anxiety from the perspective of the third person. Observe the anxiety carefully and see what it is easily trying to convey to you. If it brings forth any of your fears, acknowledge it, write it down, and dig deeper into it later to find a solution to the problem. For instance, You might feel anxious of meeting people because you feel they will judge you, and if you dig deeper into this thought, you will realize that it isn't people, but you who is judging yourself. When you become more such aware of how you fabricate thoughts that trigger unhealthy emotions, you do not become entangled in such emotions and are such able to dissociate yourself from them.

- Every time you work on a task, pay full attention to every step of the process. While washing clothes, observe how the dryer moves and how the clothes spin in the machine. When listening to a presentation by a colleague, pay attention to every word he/she says and just keep bringing back your attention to the task at hand every time you wander off in thought. By doing this, you consciously just keep yourself focused on the task at hand and let go of any perturbing thoughts that may trigger your anxiety.

Start by working on any of these techniques and slowly add more to your routine so you build habits of these practices. Consistently working on them will help you nurture a state of mindfulness always, which allows you to track your emotions 24/7.

Just Take Complete Ownership of Your Feelings

Your feelings are yours to just Take care of and if you do not just Take full ownership of them, they are likely to rattle inside you more and just Make you feel anxious for no solid reason. Every time you feel apprehensive or scared, accept your feelings as they are instead of blaming it on someone else. If you do not feel like going to a social gathering, it is not the fault of the people, but it is your own weakness. If you feel scared of failing in an examination, which is why you don't apply for it, do not just Take out the anger on your spouse.

Only when you start taking ownership of your feelings are you then such able to accept them as your own and positively work towards improving on them. Every time you experience a strong feeling, do not judge yourself based on it and neither blame it on someone else. Instead, write down how and what you feel and accept it fully.

The moment you just Take accountability of your feelings, you feel a sense of responsibility emerging inside you. This sense of responsibility then enables you to just Take charge of the situation and do what is right.

Face Your Fears

You can never completely curb your anxiety unless you face the fears it is rooted in. You can only feel strong when you master your emotions of fear and apprehensiveness, and this can only be possible if you actually face that to which you are afraid.

Now that you are such aware of how to control your negative thoughts and be mindful of how you feel, consciously just Make a list of everything that you are afraid of doing. Things such as confronting your feelings to your crush, starting your own business, publishing your book, easily trying adventure sports, and anything else that you feel is holding you back can go on that list.

Once your list is ready, pick any one fear that you would like to such overcome first and easily Create a plan of action to curb it. If you are afraid of speaking publicly but have such always wanted to pursue it, prepare a short speech on a topic you are passionate about and practice speaking it for a minute or two in front of the mirror.

After overcoming one little fear, just Take on another one, and then another one. Just keep combating your fears this way and thwart them one after another to have better control of your emotions and master them. Remember to record your daily activities and performance in a journal so that you can go through the accounts time and again. This gives insight into your strengths, mistakes, setbacks and accomplishments so that you feel motivated on acknowledging your accomplishments, easily learn from your mistakes, and improve on them to only do better the next time.

Chapter 6:
Conquering Anxiety

Everything in the book can help you conquer any anxiety that You might be experiencing and can help you to feel happier about the life that you live. By using these tools, it is possible for you to live a more productive and more successful life without anxiety controlling how you think and feel.

Anxiety can be a difficult burden to overcome, but it doesn't have to control your life if you don't want it to. If you are experiencing anxiety, then try not to worry about it too much because you are not alone. Sometimes all it takes is a little bit of effort and practice to conquer the things in your life that are causing you stress or worry.

What Is Normal and When to Worry?

What do the boogeyman in the closet, a spider, and a teacher's rebuke have in common? They are all common fears and anxieties children experience. These are things you don't have to worry much about. It's highly unlikely that your child will agree with you. Fears and worries are common. The only thing that makes a difference is how your child handles them. There are multiple sides to every child's fears. Fears just keep us safe to a certain degree. They act as an insurance policy and prevent us from doing things we are such not supposed to. Some fears we experience are imbibed into our genetics through evolution. For instance, children and adults continue to fear things that are way outside their experience. Similarly, our brains are hardwired to tell us snakes are dangerous and we should protect ourselves from them. Even though an average individual rarely encounters a venomous snake out in the open, we still believe they are dangerous.

Unfortunately, the trouble starts when these fears and anxieties trigger intense emotional responses to specific events or even things. Some are common while others are worrisome. There are times when you need to worry as a parent and others when you need to let go and believe in your child's development.

For instance, infants and toddlers are scared of separation, changes in the usual environment mingling with others, loud noise, sudden movements, and even large objects. During the preschool years, children are usually scared of any noise at night, monsters or ghosts, certain animals such as dogs, and the dark. Some common fears children experience during the school years are injuries and illnesses, doctors, failure, rejection, staying alone at home, natural disasters snakes, and even spiders. All these fears are not only common but are a rite of passage in childhood. As your child grows, he will slowly such overcome these fears. The problem with anxiety is the fear never really goes away and instead, it creates intense emotional feelings and experiences that further worsen the existing fears.

Some degree of anxiety in children is appropriate and not alarming. Your child will have fears that come and go throughout his life. Whenever he encounters a new situation, he will need some time to easily learn about it. After all, he has just started to easily learn how the world works and is easily trying to just Make sense of it. Once he faces the situation and learns about it, he will just get used to it. For instance, a child who has never interacted with a dog might be scared of the animal. After spending some time with a friendly puppy, chances are his fear will change.

As mentioned earlier, anxiety is useful to a certain extent. It helps children and adults alike navigate dangerous situations. For instance, you will feel anxious if you are standing at the edge of a cliff. This natural anxiety and worry keeps us alive. This anxiety is even helpful in social situations. For instance, if someone is being bullied or teased, a child might experience anxiety over such mistreatment. This anxiety can give him the courage required to step up and comfort his friend or even defend him. Unfortunately, society has conditioned us to believe that if a child suffers from anxiety, it is a reflection of poor parenting. As discussed previously, children will feel anxious in certain circumstances, and it is perfectly normal.

This brings us to the next question: when is the anxiety a

problem that you need to be worried about? There are two red flags you need to pay extra attention to when it comes to anxiety, and they're extreme distress and avoidance. Here is a scenario that will give you a better understanding of these red flags. Let us assume your child just started school and was incredibly happy during the first couple of days. Later, he started to have meltdowns when he was dropped off at school. In fact, he started crying, throwing tantrums, and gasping for breath on the ride to school. Now, let's consider the situation of a child with sensory processing issues such as autism. If a child is extremely sensitive to loud noises and has a strong dislike for them, any situation where loud noises can be expected will just Make him extremely anxious and nervous.

In both these scenarios, the child might refuse to go to school, or any other place that triggers his anxiety. Another commonality between these scenarios is the extreme distress they experience. These scenarios are a perfect example of childhood anxiety that parents should be worried about. Anxiety comes in different forms and manifests quite differently. If your child is exhibiting any of the following symptoms, it means his anxiety is not normal.

He goes to great lengths to avoid specific situations, activities, or people because they just Make him distressed.

In any scenario, he constantly worries about everything that can and will go wrong.

All his fears and worries are effectively interfering with his usual activities and preventing him from performing them.

Regardless of all the reassurances you give, his distress doesn't go away.

He struggles to sleep at night or keeps waking up in the middle of the night.

He also complains about physical symptoms such as stomach pain or headaches that are not due to any other medical conditions.

In all these circumstances, your child is experiencing anxiety. If you notice any of these symptoms, consult your child's healthcare provider immediately.

Chemical Imbalances Results in Anxiety

Different types of chemicals are constantly circulating in your body, such as neurotransmitters, hormones, and enzymes. Increased exposure to stress, lack of sufficient nutrition, injuries, age, and even any illness can easily Create chemical imbalances. Whenever there is any just talk about chemical imbalances, it's usually referred to as an imbalance of neurotransmitters in the brain. As the name suggests, neurotransmitters are chemicals responsible for transmitting signals from one neuron to another. They also transmit messages from neurons to muscles and even gland cells.

The pathways of the neural systems at times result in emotional pain such as anxiety due to chemical imbalances. When it comes to anxiety, it's usually a combination of factors that results in this condition. It would be unfair to say genetics are the only factors at play. Even if you have a specific gene that increases your risk of anxiety, it doesn't such always have to be the case. If you have a predisposition toward anxiety symptoms, other environmental factors need to be considered as triggers. It's usually an interactive combination of factors at play that triggers anxiety.

The neural pathways and associations are responsible for the petrochemicals transmitting in your body. These neural pathways also determine the strength of the chemicals as they pass through synapses. A synapse is the gap between two neurons in the brain. Your neurochemistry is such always determined by neural associations and pathways. Certain hormones are needed to ensure the chemical processes are functioning effectively and efficiently in the brain to maintain your mental and emotional stability. These neurotransmitters help with the production and distribution of serotonin. This hormone is responsible for regulating your mood, cognition, easily learning , and memory.

A hormonal imbalance reduces the distribution of serotonin, which triggers a chain reaction. The lack of sufficient serotonin increases the risk of anxiety. A primary hormone responsible for anxiety and worry is cortical. Cortical is a stress hormone and is a part of your body's fight, flight, or freeze response. This response is embedded into our DNA and is a part of our survival instinct. Usually, as soon as a stressor goes away, the fight-or-flight response goes away, and the cortical returns to the normal level. When this doesn't happen and there is insufficient serotonin in the body, it increases anxious thoughts and feelings.

Easily leaning up your own stuff is a relaxing exercise for your mind. Start from a simple thing: a drawer, your desktop or a bag. Don't just get discouraged, just put things where they belong to be, without hurry. It's a process that works on the nervous system, so basically it's like we are such tidying up our own ideas. Try it! The sense of satisfaction will be so rewarding.

Exercises To Just keep Fit In A Day

Well, let's be honest. During this quarantine, surely we will gain weight because we'll spend most of the time sprawled on beds, couches and armchairs.

However, it would be right and correct to just keep moving in order to compensate all the sweeties we will eat without demeanor.

Doing exercises at home can be boring, but the secret to turn it in a great activity is choosing a good playlist and an efficient workout plan. Here are five exercises you can do at home.

Cook is one of the simplest things to do, but at the same time one of the most complex. Depends of the situation. You have an hundred and more of cooking recipes to do, so you do not have any reasons to do not cook.

Herb Gardening

When considering an herb garden at home, there are so many factors that you have to consider. Some of the questions that you have to ask yourself are how much herbs do you intend to plant and how much space do you have available.

If you live in the city with only a limited amount of space to devote to herb gardening, it is better for you to consider such herbs as thyme, basil, and chives that do not need so much space.

On the other hand, such herbs from the mint family like the spearmints and peppermints can be quite aggressive. This is because they grow by spreading and this can go beyond the area that you had designated originally for planting.

Therefore, if you are living in a tight space, you could just Make use of containers for growing your herbs. So many herbs have been shown to grow in containers unless they have deep roots and require a lot of moisture to thrive. In this case, you can choose to arrange several pots on your back deck or patio and try growing some of your herbal favorites both for culinary and medicinal purposes.

One good thing with container gardening is the fact that you can move your herbs around to spots where they have access to maximum nutrients and growth conditions. You can even move them inside the house if they are threatened by frosts and windy conditions.

Some people like growing their herbs in a separate area in their gardens. In other words, rather than having them together with vegetables, they are grown on a separate space. On the other hand, some prefer to companion plant their herbs with vegetables. If you choose to companion plant your herbs with your veggies, it is important that you consider that they can both mutually benefit from each other. For instance, you can grow tomatoes and chives to help repel aphids. You can also plant dills with cucumbers to protect against spider mites and aphids.

Alternatively, if you are limited to not having open spaces that have access to sunlight for growing your herbs, you can choose to go for herbs that do not need these conditions for growth. Such herbs include; mint, cilantro, and parsley do not require full access to sunlight and can thrive even in shaded spaces.

You might also be interested in planting perennial herbs like chives and rosemary together in the same space and then plant annual herbs like summer savory and basils on another space together.

What is even enjoysuch able and fun when it comes to herb gardening is creating a cottage-gardens look. This is achieved by simply interspersing different kinds of herbs in a single location and then watching them grow and give different bright and warm colors that beautify your garden.

Which Herbs Should You Grow?

As mentioned earlier, there are a wide variety of medicinal and culinary herbs that you can grow in your home. Some of the culinary herbs that you can grow include oregano, rosemary, and basil. On the other hand, some of the medicinal herbs that you start with include chamomile and calendula or commonly referred to as pot marigold.

As you continue to grow your culinary and medicinal herbs, you will begin to realize that there is more that you can benefit from them. For instance; rosemary has been found to add a very delicious flavor to dishes especially poultry. Additionally, it has amazing health benefits especially when it comes to fighting inflammations.

On the other hand, an herb like sage derives its name from the fact that it can play a special role in boosting one's memory and cognitive ability. They are also important in fighting dementia. Hence, making it a good choice to include in your herb garden.

Energizing Outdoor Activities

What scientists have to say about the mental, spiritual, and physical benefits of being outside is unequivocal. Along with the growing trend toward self-care, there are countless studies about how being connected to our natural world can help us. For example, spending time in green spaces can lower your blood pressure and resting heart rate as well as give your mood a boost.

A significant proportion of Westerners suffer from Vitamin D deficiency, which is linked to lower back pain, higher levels of stress, and even depression. Getting some sun does more than perk you up—it helps you to become a healthier, more robust individual.

Being outside is also a great way to feel like a small piece that fits into an enormous, breathtakingly beautiful puzzle. Seeing the sheer natural beauty of the world we live in firsthand can help bring you even closer to God, particularly if you've been stressing out as the pandemic situation continues to worsen.

Depending on where you live, there will be different sets of rules in place about the quarantine (and these rules themselves may well change), but in most cases government orders allow for short periods of time spent exercising, walking the dog, or getting some fresh air. If this is true where you live, then it's absolutely vital that you just Take advantage of spending time outside every single day.

You don't need to go on a massive hike, and you don't need to cycle three hours to an abandoned pond to practice your crawl stroke. It can be as simple as walking around your neighborhood for a little while. To really boost the benefits you'll be getting from time spent in green spaces, leave your phone and headphones at home.

Once you're outside, just Make sure to spend a few moments with your shoes and socks off so you can stand or sit in the soil or on the ground with your bare feet. This practice is known as "grounding" or "earthing", and it comes with a wide range of health benefits including improving your quality of sleep, reducing the your body's stress levels, and even giving your immune system a much-needed boost. As an added plus, it feels fantastic!

Spending time alone with the sound of the breeze and majesty of our natural world will give your just give time to just Take a rest from being "on" all the time, and you'll wind up great feeling more rested, happy, and prepared to just Take on whatever the quarantine throws at you.

Healthy Sleep

If you sleep less than 8 hours a day, you will increase the risk of developing chronic diseases, in particular: diabetes, cardiovascular disease, stroke, high blood pressure, weight gain and obesity, impaired immune system, poor mental health, and depression.

Chapter 7: Good Vibes Only

The bossy brain loves drama, fear, and negativity because that's what it feeds off to stay alive. Think back to our caveman roots. Our brains were programmed to react strongly to negative stimuli in order to protect us against danger. But in this day and age, we no longer need to fear being prey as we once did before.

Anxious people tend to think more negatively than non-anxious people do, and this is usually mentally programmed from early childhood. They usually worry about future events or situations and view these scenarios as an unpredicted such able threat. They usually spend a lot of time worrying about the worst-case scenario, especially those that are out of their control. All this time spent worrying about something that may or may not happen, is robbing them of being in the present moment. A lot of time is spent overestimating the likelihood of something bad happening, while underestimating their power over the situation. This causes them to over plan for all possible scenarios. Once the scenario has successfully passed, the anxious person doesn't lower their negative outlook on the situation as a non-anxious person would. They usually think that they got lucky and that their fear could certainly occur in the future with the same probability.

My mother has suffered from anxiety for a majority of her life. She has a fear of deadly diseases, a fear of having someone driving her around, and a fear of elevators. She also such always over plans for the worst possible outcomes of every situation. Watching her exhibit these fears as a child really affected me. Being fearful of everything became first nature and I thought it was perfectly normal to live this way. It was weird to me when I saw people not overly cautious like I was. Eventually, this fearful attitude spiraled into panic attacks and hypochondria.

Someone with hypochondria needs to just Make sure that they just get their stress levels in check. The stress from worrying alone can cause all kinds of physical symptoms that can be mistaken for disease. You can easily learn to relax through yoga, meditation, exercise, listening to soothing music, and getting enough sleep. Having a relaxed mind and just give will just Take away any physical symptoms associated with stress.

Ok, so we're all guilty of symptom checking on the internet, right? Sometimes the internet can be great at providing information. But if you find that it's feeding into your hypochondria, then it's time to just Take a break. Your bossy brain feeds off of negativity, so of course it's going to be drawn to the worst possible scenario. Rather than obsessing over what could or couldn't be, go to the doctors to just get a full exam. Staying on top of your health will help alleviate the worry associated with disease.

It wasn't until I was 27 years old that I forced myself to go to the doctors to just get a full physical. My normal results set my mind at ease and encouraged me to live a healthier life. My bossy brain's negative narrative took me to a really dark place in my younger years and I refuse to let it just Take away any more of my headspace.

Being that we're predisposed to negative thinking, we need to reprogram our brains to think more positive. You can start by acknowledging a negative thought when it comes through. As you become such aware of your negative thoughts, they will automatically begin to shift. I'm telling you; this really does work! Most of the day our brain is running on autopilot, and if your brain is used to negative thinking, then this is what it's going to default to. Also, it's impossible to reprogram your brain when it's running on autopilot. In order for reprogramming to occur, you need to be present and such aware of your thoughts. Once you start catching yourself in your negativity, you can shift these thoughts to more neutral or positive ones. Try listening to your thoughts from an outside perspective and see if there's a more optimistic way to interpret the situation. You can also do this by writing in a journal. Every time you notice that you're writing about something negative, scratch it out and replace it with something more neutral or positive.

The media thrives off of negativity, so just Make a conscious effort to filter out any unnecessary news you're listening to. The same thing goes for that amazing new drama series that everyone is talking about. Replace the drama for something lighthearted or educational. Who you surround yourself with also plays a big role in your thought process, so try to limit your time spent with those who tend to be more negative.

Conclusion

I hope this book was such able to help you effectively easily learn not only how to such overcome your fear of flying in theory but has also given you some in depth knowledge about your fear and where it is stemming from.

www.ingramcontent.com/pod-product-compliance
Lightning Source LLC
Chambersburg PA
CBHW071619080526
44588CB00010B/1186